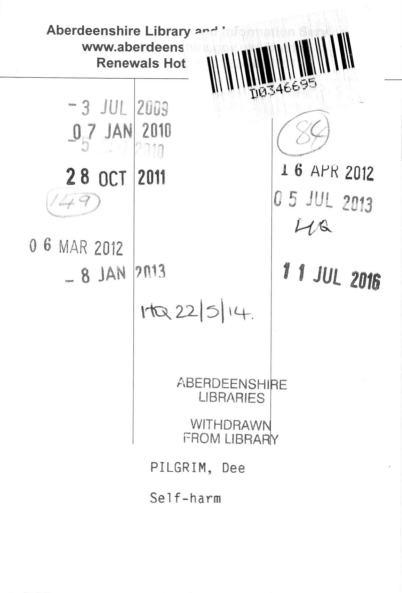

PILGRIM, Dee

Self-harm

REAL LIFE ISSUES

Real Life Issues are self-help guides offering information and advice on a range of key issues that matter to teenagers. Each book defines the issue, probes the reader's experience of it and offers ways of understanding and coping with it. Written in a lively and accessible style, *Real Life Issues* aim to demystify the areas that teenagers find hard to talk about, providing honest facts, practical advice, inspirational quotes, positive reassurance, and guidance towards specialist help.

Other titles in the series include:

Real Life Issues: Addictions
Real Life Issues: Bullying
Real Life Issues: Confidence & Self-Esteem
Real Life Issues: Coping with Life
Real Life Issues: Eating Disorders
Real Life Issues: Family Break-ups
Real Life Issues: Money
Real Life Issues: Prejudice
Real Life Issues: Sex & Relationships
Real Life Issues: Stress

REAL LIFE ISSUES:
SELF-HARM

Dee Pilgrim

Real Life Issues: Self-Harm
This first edition published in 2007 by Trotman an imprint of Crimson Publishing,
Westminster House, Kew Road, Richmond, Surrey TW9 2ND
www.crimsonpublishing.co.uk

© Trotman 2007

Editorial and Publishing Team
Author Dee Pilgrim
Editorial Mina Patria, Publishing Director; Jo Jacomb, Editorial Manager;
Ian Turner, Production Editor
Production John O'Toole, Operations Manager
Advertising Tom Lee, Commercial Director

Designed by XAB

British Library Cataloguing in Publication Data
A catalogue record for this book is available from the British Library

ISBN 978 1 84455 116 3

Typeset by Photoprint, Torquay
Printed and bound in Great Britain by
Creative Print & Design, Wales

CONTENTS:

vii   About the Author

ix   Acknowledgements

1   INTRODUCTION
What this book is all about

6   **1.** DIFFERENT TYPES OF SELF-HARM
The ways people harm themselves

15   **2.** UNDERSTANDING WHY IT HAPPENS
The reasons why people harm themselves

22   **3.** HOW TO SPOT A SELF-HARMER
Clues to show if people around you are self-harming

28   **4.** STOPPING THE CYCLE OF SELF-HARM
Practical ways to help yourself or others stop self-harming

37   **5.** WHO CAN I TURN TO?
Where to get information and advice

49   **6.** THE ROAD TO RECOVERY
Breaking the cycle and moving on

57   CONCLUSION

60   RESOURCES

REAL LIFE ISSUES:
Self-Harm

ABOUT THE AUTHOR

Dee Pilgrim completed the pre-entry, periodical journalism course at the London College of Printing before working on a variety of music and women's titles. She has written numerous articles and interviews for *Company*, *Cosmopolitan*, *New Woman*, *Woman's Journal* and *Weight Watchers* magazines. For many years she covered new output by singer/songwriters for *Top* magazine, which was distributed via Tower Records stores, and during this period interviewed the likes of Tori Amos, Tom Robinson and Joan Armatrading. As a freelancer for Independent Magazines she concentrated on celebrity interviews and film, theatre and restaurant reviews for magazines such as *Ms London*, *Girl About Town*, *LAM* and *Nine to Five*, and in her capacity as a critic she has appeared on both radio and television. She is currently the film reviewer for *Now* magazine and has written a number of titles for Trotman. When not attending film screenings she is active in the Critics' Circle and is the secretary for its film section.

REAL LIFE ISSUES:
Self-Harm

ACKNOWLEDGEMENTS

There are many people I wish to thank for their help and input, as this has probably been the hardest book I have ever written. For practical information on the issue, thanks to Mind, the Royal College of Nursing, the Mental Health Foundation and everyone who participated in the *Truth Hurts* report. A very special thank you goes to the many anonymous young people who have confided their thoughts on their own self-harming and recuperation: you will find these dotted among the text. Finally, I am very grateful to Max O'Neill, Senior Lecturer in Psychology at the University of East London, for sharing his expertise on the subject so clearly and with such compassion.

INTRODUCTION
What this book is all about

'On the outside I know people think I'm fine, but they don't know what it's like on the inside: the pain, the rage, the self-hate and the guilt. That's why I self-harm: I cut myself in order to let all this poison out. It's my release and it helps me to survive.'

Our teenage years can be a troubled time. The transition between childhood and maturity can seem like an uphill struggle: rampaging hormones change our bodies, and awakening sexuality brings startling thoughts. Our body shape is transformed. If we're boys our voices break, girls boast new curves, body hair starts growing in strange places and the dreaded acne can develop regardless of gender. Meanwhile, outside influences can be even more trying as we enter a new and often frightening world. Responsibilities we have never encountered before force us to grow up quickly and put new pressures on us.

All of this affects teenagers in different ways. Some seem relatively unconcerned by it all, but others can be profoundly disturbed and unable to cope with the situation. For some the pressure inside builds up so much that they have to find a way to let it escape, a safety valve that stops them blowing up. For more and more young people that safety valve comes in the form of self-harm.

WHAT IS IT?

According to NICE (the National Institute for Clinical Excellence) self-harm is 'an expression of personal distress, usually made in private, by an individual who hurts him or herself.' Childline defines self-harm as 'when people set out to harm themselves deliberately, sometimes in a hidden way. Self-harm can include cutting, burning, bruising or poisoning, but does not usually mean that someone wants to commit suicide.'

Whatever the definition, the fact is that self-harm is becoming more common throughout society, but most especially among young people: and that should give us all cause for concern. If you have never self-harmed or don't know (or think you don't know) anyone who does, the thought of a person deliberately hurting him or herself may seem alien, even unbelievable. We spend so much time protecting ourselves from things that might harm us, why on earth would we inflict injury on our own bodies?

Because it goes against what we perceive to be instinctive methods of survival (fight, flight and self-protection) self-harm has long been a taboo subject. Self-harmers often feel guilty about what they do so they don't tell anyone. This makes assessing the size of the problem difficult, but recent research shows that a growing number of young people find that self-harm is the only way they can cope with an emotional pain that threatens to overwhelm them.

According to *Truth Hurts*, the report of the National Enquiry into Self-Harm Among Young People in the UK (Mental Health Foundation, 2006), 1 in 15 young people have self-harmed. In other words, in every secondary school classroom there will be, on average, two young people who have hurt themselves as a response to the pressures of growing up. The average age at which a young person self-harms is now as low as 12 years. This is a serious public health problem – it is estimated that about 25,000 young people are admitted to hospital in the UK each year after deliberately harming themselves.

Another concern is that a small minority of people who self-harm will also try to kill themselves. Although young women aged between 15 and 19 are most likely to attempt suicide, young men are much more likely to die as a result of a suicide attempt. While the majority of self-harmers are girls (Childline gets 12 times as many girls calling about self-harming as boys), the number of young men who hurt themselves is growing and the suicide rate in young men has doubled since 1985.

These figures probably represent only the tip of the iceberg, because so many self-harmers do not admit to what they are doing. 'It is done behind closed doors. It is their little secret, their little ritual,' says Max O'Neill, Senior Lecturer in Psychology at the University of East London. A counselling psychologist for the last six years, he has been involved in a number of research projects, including Listening to Young People, and says we must see the whole subject as a reflection of the society in which we now live. 'It is happening because of low self-esteem, huge amounts of pressure to succeed, expectations of parents, continual assessment at school and bullying. We are facing a huge epidemic in binge-drinking, we know eating disorders are on the increase and we know there are increasing problems with adolescents and drugs, especially cannabis.'

We live in an aspirational society in which everything and everyone has to be better, more successful and richer than ever before. This 'need to succeed' puts a strain on almost everybody, but particularly on young people: they are the future of our society, so they carry all its hopes and expectations on their shoulders. For many this is a burden they simply cannot bear and they buckle under the strain. 'What they believe is being asked of them and their abilities, and even their own expectations, are impossible to reach,' says Max O'Neill. 'They believe they will never be good enough and self-harming is a way they cope with that belief. But self-harm is not a particularly healthy way of coping with stress and anxiety. It is only a momentary release for the pressure and does not address the fundamental psychological causes that make these young people want to self-harm.'

This book will look in detail at the many reasons why young people hurt themselves, to give them and those around them a better understanding of their behaviour and some ideas about practical ways to change it. If you are a person who self-harms this book will:

▪ show you are not alone
▪ explain how others have coped with their self-harming
▪ give you strategies to help you minimise or even stop your self-harm
▪ tell you where and who to turn to for help
▪ give you hope for a harm-free future.

Because it is so secretive and taboo, many people find talking about self-harming very difficult – they feel uncomfortable and unable to handle the idea. This is mainly because of ignorance about the subject – they simply don't know what to do or what to say. If you are a friend or a family member of someone who self-harms (or who you suspect may be self-harming) this book will:

- explain exactly what self-harm is
- give you a better understanding of why people self-harm
- help you spot the warning signs of someone who is self-harming
- show you how you can help self-harmers to help themselves
- give advice on organisations you can turn to
- help you to talk about the subject openly and freely.

In recent months there has been more media coverage of the subject and there are now many websites devoted to it. Some health professionals are very wary of some of these websites because they feel they 'glamorise' self-harm ('some people see it as quite trendy,' says Max O'Neill) and may encourage more young people to 'copycat' self-harming behaviour. However, there is no research to suggest that this is true. Knowledge is power, and the more we know about self-harm and the more we understand why it happens, the more we can do to tackle its root causes. Until we do so, continuing generations of young people will grow up mentally and physically scarred by the pressure and stress of modern society and the far from ideal mechanism they have found that enables them to cope.

'I got used to this being my way of coping with things. I honestly didn't feel there was any other way.'

CHAPTER ONE:

DIFFERENT TYPES OF SELF-HARM
The ways people harm themselves

'I start to feel more in control the minute I see the blood.'

At times we all display self-destructive behaviours, even if we don't think of them as such – drinking too much, taking needless physical risks or comfort eating. However, for most of us this behaviour will not develop into full-blown self-harming. Some people may only self-harm a few times during particularly stressful periods, such as before exams or when breaking up with a girlfriend or boyfriend, and once this period is over the self-harm stops. But for others it becomes a regular occurrence and feels like the only way they can cope with what they are feeling.

For about 70% of self-harmers, injuring themselves is a single episode triggered by a stressful situation and they stop self-harming once the triggering situation is resolved. However, for about 30% it is continuous and recurrent, and symptomatic of more long-term psychological problems. While most of us look after ourselves by eating well, exercising and learning relaxation techniques to deal with stress, for self-harmers physically abusing their bodies is their way of looking after themselves – it's not about wanting to end their lives, it's about trying to stay alive.

People self-harm in many ways, including:

- taking overdoses
- abusing alcohol, tobacco or drugs
- ingesting poisonous substances or placing items inside the body
- pulling out hair or eyelashes
- abusing food by starving or over-eating
- deliberately throwing themselves against hard surfaces
- burning their skin
- scratching or picking at their skin, causing sores
- cutting the skin.

In the box on the next page is some information on the Australian Mental Health Triage Scale, which doctors and nurses use to assess the level of severity of injuries displayed by self-harmers when they arrive at hospital emergency departments – and which NICE recommends should also be used in the UK. It shows just how broad the term 'self-harm' is. Callers contacting Childline have also talked about harming their bodies by deliberate bruising, banging their heads against a wall, falling over and, in at least one instance, purposely breaking a limb.

Although this chapter does contain information on other forms of self-harm, such as eating disorders, it mainly deals with the injuries most usually associated with self-harm, for example cutting, burning or scratching the skin.

Interestingly, Max O'Neill says there do seem to be links between the way people harm themselves and their gender. 'Certainly, the boys I

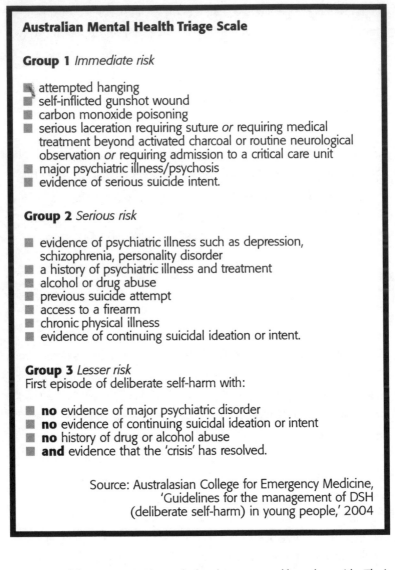

Australian Mental Health Triage Scale

Group 1 *Immediate risk*

- attempted hanging
- self-inflicted gunshot wound
- carbon monoxide poisoning
- serious laceration requiring suture *or* requiring medical treatment beyond activated charcoal or routine neurological observation *or* requiring admission to a critical care unit
- major psychiatric illness/psychosis
- evidence of serious suicide intent.

Group 2 *Serious risk*

- evidence of psychiatric illness such as depression, schizophrenia, personality disorder
- a history of psychiatric illness and treatment
- alcohol or drug abuse
- previous suicide attempt
- access to a firearm
- chronic physical illness
- evidence of continuing suicidal ideation or intent.

Group 3 *Lesser risk*
First episode of deliberate self-harm with:

- **no** evidence of major psychiatric disorder
- **no** evidence of continuing suicidal ideation or intent
- **no** history of drug or alcohol abuse
- **and** evidence that the 'crisis' has resolved.

Source: Australasian College for Emergency Medicine,
'Guidelines for the management of DSH
(deliberate self-harm) in young people,' 2004

interviewed for my research tended to be more reckless than girls. Their self-harming seemed to be much more related to drugs and alcohol or taking risks around sexual behaviour than was true of the girls, who tended to self-harm through abuse of food and cutting themselves.'

EATING DISORDERS

If you have a low opinion of yourself and lack self-esteem – as most self-harmers do – you probably think there's not much point in taking care of your physical or mental well being. Instead, you may abuse food by starving yourself (anorexia), or overeating and then vomiting (bulimia).

Until recently both anorexia and bulimia were seen as problems primarily affecting girls, but more boys are now being diagnosed with eating disorders. 'We underestimated the cases of eating disorders in boys,' concedes Max O'Neill. 'Boys always did it – we just didn't hear about it – but now it is more acceptable for boys to talk about these things, which is why we see more coming forward.'

Anorexics and bulimics take very serious risks with their health. As they mature they can develop problems with bone density and fertility; and both conditions can lead to premature death. Eating disorders are covered in depth in another Trotman title, *Real Life Issues: Eating Disorders* (see the Resources section at the end of this book).

SUBSTANCE ABUSE

The teen years are often seen as a time of experimentation when many young men and women try recreational drugs, such as alcohol, tobacco and cannabis, for the first time. However, while the occasional drink is seen as socially acceptable, the growing number of teenagers binge-drinking or taking classified drugs is a cause for concern for everyone.

This is mainly for two reasons. First, young people tend to use a greater quantity of their drug of choice than was the case in the past, and this in turn increases the risk of major organ damage and accidental overdose. Second, many young people start drinking, smoking and/or taking drugs at an earlier age than ever before: and younger bodies cope less well with the side effects of these substances.

While alcohol and substance abuse are five times more common in men than in women (with young males accounting for 70–80% of solvent abuse – sniffing glue or other substances) the gap between the genders is closing rapidly.

Alcohol

Britain has one of the highest rates of binge-drinking among young people. The Institute of Alcohol Studies found that over a quarter of all 15- and 16-year-olds go on three or more drinking binges a month. According to the NHS, the number of children admitted to hospital because of alcohol abuse has jumped by more than 20% in the last five years.

Many young people say they like drinking because it makes them feel more confident socially and it helps them to lose their inhibitions. But what it really does is mask their unhappiness or inability to cope with life – and their problems are still there (along with an almighty hangover) when they sober up. Drinking too much alcohol has other serious consequences: it affects your ability to assess risk, makes you more accident-prone and aggressive (which means you're more likely to get into fights), and can permanently damage your liver.

> The number of under-18s admitted to hospital with alcohol-related conditions rose from 6288 in 2000/2001 to 7579 in 2004/2005. Up to 20 youngsters a day are diagnosed with conditions ranging from alcohol poisoning to excessive drinking causing behavioural disorders.

Tobacco

The health dangers of smoking tobacco are well known. Young lungs are very susceptible to the carcinogens (chemicals that cause cancer) in tobacco smoke – which is why the government has produced advertisements urging adults to stop smoking around children. Smoking a cigarette can only ever be a momentary distraction. It may take your mind off your problems for a few minutes, but when you stub out that cigarette the problems will still be there. Tobacco is highly addictive and it is better never to have smoked in the first place than to have to try to quit.

Cannabis

After alcohol and tobacco, cannabis is the third most popular drug of choice for teenagers. Studies in the UK show that two in five 15-year-olds have tried cannabis – more than in any other country in Europe. According to the Home Office, in 2004 11% of schoolchildren aged between 11 and 15 used cannabis. This is worrying because the younger you start using cannabis the greater the risk that it will trigger psychosis or lead to serious mental illness.

Professor Peter Jones of Cambridge University, who contributed to the report, says children who start smoking cannabis at the age of 10 or 11 are three times more likely to develop schizophrenia than children who do not use it. Although cannabis is a euphoric drug – it gives you a 'high' – it can also lead to psychotic episodes, involving hallucinations, fantasies and a sense of losing touch with reality, which may last for weeks and can be very frightening. Cannabis was reclassified from a Class B drug to the lower status Class C drug in 2004 but it is now expected to return to Class B status with tougher penalties for possession.

Ecstasy

Another recreational drug popular among teenagers, with up to 5% of 16- to 24-year-olds using it, is Ecstasy, or E. Recent research shows that as little as six tablets of E can cause brain damage, so even small amounts of the drug should not be considered safe. E is thought to be responsible for up to 50 deaths a year.

SELF-POISONING

Self-poisoning is when a person takes an overdose of a drug such as paracetamol, or ingests a toxic substance such as lighter fuel, paint or methylated spirits. Most people who are taken to emergency departments after overdosing have taken an over-the-counter medication, or drugs prescribed for them or others.

Although self-poisoning is far less common than other forms of self-harm it attracts more attention because self-poisoners are more likely to need and to seek medical intervention. We tend to associate self-poisoning more with attempted suicide than self-harm. About 5000 people commit suicide in Britain every year, but more than 20 times that number go to hospital following a self-harming episode. Some research done in 2004 suggests that between 40 and 100 times more young people have engaged in some form of self-harm than those who have actually gone on to end their own lives.

PULLING OUT HAIR OR EYELASHES/SCRATCHING OR PICKING AT THE SKIN

TV presenter Gail Porter lost all her hair through stress, a condition known as alopecia. When hair is lost by continuously pulling or plucking at it the condition is known as **trichotillomania**. This condition affects twice as many females as males and can occur at any time of life, but it is most common in childhood and adolescence. The hair is often pulled out in distinct patches or patterns on the scalp and some individuals also pull out eyebrows and eyelashes. Because the results are so obvious it can be extremely distressing for the sufferer, who may already have low self-esteem. The treatment for trichotillomania often involves counselling or another form of therapy.

Some people continually and obsessively pick at and scratch their skin until sores appear. They do this even when their skin isn't actually irritated or itchy, and this condition is known as **neurotic excoriation**. This can also be extremely distressing because the areas of skin affected are those easily accessed by the hands and nails, such as the face, neck and arms, and treatment will again involve some sort of psychological counselling.

BURNING OR CUTTING THE SKIN

People suffering from neurotic excoriation are usually aware of what they are doing and acknowledge their behaviour because they want to stop. This is different from the self-harmers who **cut** or **burn** their skin in private and who feel so guilty about it they often deny their behaviour. This condition is known as **dermatitis artefacta**. Injuries to the skin can be caused by:

- cutting it with fingernails or a knife, razorblade or other sharp instrument
- burning it with a flame, for example with cigarettes, matches or candles
- burning it with caustic chemicals, such as bleach.

Cutting is the most common form of self-harm disclosed by young people calling Childline. Sixty-two per cent of children counselled by

Childline about self-harm told counsellors that they had cut themselves. Their behaviour often takes the form of a ritual – they have a 'special' instrument for cutting themselves, which they may keep hidden with other self-harming paraphernalia such as sterile gauze strips and antiseptic ointment. Often the self-harmer feels no pain, but a sense of physical release, as they cut and burn. This is because serotonin and other chemicals in the brain that are released when a person feels in danger, or when the body is injured, bring a feeling of calm and well being.

Although not initially life-threatening, cutting can cause deep scars both emotionally and physically. If the self-harm continues for some time without being addressed it may also become more serious, as Max O'Neill explains: 'Working clinically I have seen that often a person starts to cut deeper if the self-harming continues. This is because the release they get from the cutting gets less and less each time they do it. They compensate for this sometimes by increasing the frequency of the cutting, or by making the cuts deeper, and that is obviously very dangerous especially when the cutting gets closer to major blood vessels.'

All these forms of self-harm come about because the self-harmer is in deep distress. He or she is suffering from an emotional pain they have no other way of dealing with. The next chapter explores the many reasons why people feel compelled to harm themselves.

CHAPTER TWO

UNDERSTANDING WHY IT HAPPENS
The reasons why people harm themselves

'Everything was bottled up inside me, until I thought I was going to explode, but when I cut my arm and I saw the blood the pressure went away.'

Self-harmers injure themselves in order to cope with a mental anguish they feel they have no other way of dealing with. Their distress gets so unbearable they have to find some form of release and, for them, injuring their bodies is that release. 'Often my patients use similar words such as pain, pressure, build up, too much and then relief and release,' says Max O'Neill. 'They talk about seeing a red film in front of their eyes and as they cut seeing that red drain from their eyes because they are taking control back from the pressure.' On the next page is a diagram of how the cycle of self-harm works.

As Max O'Neill says, for some young people self-harming may be the only thing in their lives over which they feel they have any control. 'Self-harmers often feel guilty and the guilt just taps into their own

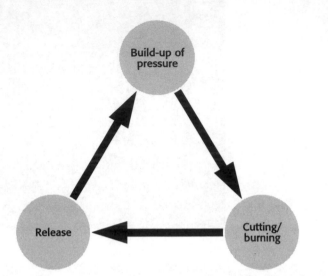

negative belief system. They think they are a bad person, an unlovable person and that negative belief system becomes self-perpetuating. The only way they can get rid of those feelings is through self-harm, that is their way of taking control. Often their lives are quite chaotic and they don't feel they have control over them but at least they can control this,' he says.

Others visualise the blood from their wounds carrying away the bad feelings they have inside themselves. It is as if cutting is a form of cleansing, and although some self-harmers do not feel pain as they injure themselves others welcome any pain they do experience because they feel dead or numb inside and the pain makes them feel more alive.

Many self-harmers have a 'trigger' for episodes of self-harming – an event or a feeling that starts to build up pressure. Each person's trigger is personal to them but most are linked to a difficult or painful experience they have had in the past or are having now, or to the anniversaries of painful experiences. According to the *Truth Hurts* report these experiences can range from being bullied or the pressure to perform well in exams (the number of people contacting self-harm websites rises significantly just before exam time), to sexual abuse or losing a loved one.

Once again, there are differences between the genders. Research carried out for *Truth Hurts* showed that young men are more likely to self-harm if: a family member has attempted suicide or deliberately harmed themselves during their lifetime; they have used drugs in the last year; and/or if they have a low self-image and low self-esteem.

Among girls the factors are: a family member or close friend who has attempted suicide or deliberately harmed themselves; a low self-image and low self-esteem; cigarette smoking in the past week; drug use in the past year; worries about sexual orientation; high impulsivity; and/or a high anxiety level.

The most frequent reasons given by teenagers for their self-harming are:

- being bullied at school
- not getting on with parents
- stress and worry about academic performance and exams
- parental divorce
- bereavement
- unwanted pregnancy
- experience of abuse in earlier childhood (sexual, physical and/or emotional)
- difficulties associated with sexuality
- problems to do with race, culture or religion
- low self-esteem
- feelings of being rejected.

Other external factors include:

- a parent who has mental health problems
- a parent who is addicted to drugs
- a serious illness or being taken into hospital
- being made homeless
- being taken into care.

BEING BULLIED

In 2005 Bullying Online carried out a survey of more than 8500 children, parents and teachers. It found that 30% of the children had felt suicidal after being bullied at school.

Every day some 20,000 British youngsters skip school because they are being bullied, and a third of all truancy cases are a result of pupils being too scared to go to school. Bullying seriously undermines self-confidence and can make people afraid to tell anyone about what is happening to them: and with no one to confide in, self-harm may be the only way they have of showing the pain they feel inside. If you or someone you know has been or is being bullied, have a look at Chapter 5 for some information on the many groups that can offer help and support.

BEING ABUSED

When a young person is abused – whether emotionally, physically or sexually – by someone close to them they often blame themselves and feel guilty, their rationale being 'I love and trust this person, so it must be my fault' or 'I must have done something bad for this to happen.' They may also feel shame and self-hatred, and so self-harming acts as a form of self-punishment. Children who have been abused by a grown-up may find it difficult to trust an adult again, so they often won't talk about their experiences to people in authority.

Because the experience is so traumatic many people deny the abuse has taken place or suppress the memories, and self-harming becomes the only way they can express their pain.

BEREAVEMENT

Losing someone you love through an accident, illness or suicide can be a shattering experience, and it really does seem as though there is a hole in your life, a space that no one else can fill. More than half of those who have lost loved ones have suicidal thoughts, and between 17% and 25% will experience some form of depressive illness in the first year after the death. A death may be the trigger for a young person to start self-harming.

If you have been bereaved and are finding it difficult to cope, another Trotman title, *Real Life Issues: Bereavement* offers advice and strategies to help (see the Resources section at the end of this book). American research has shown that if the death is caused by suicide the survivors are more likely to commit suicide too. No one is exactly sure why this is the case, but if you have been affected by suicide and are in turn feeling suicidal – or if you have a friend in that situation – you might find it useful to look at Mind's excellent booklet, *How to Help Someone Who is Feeling Suicidal* (see the Resources section).

DIVORCE/FAMILY PROBLEMS

It's a sad fact of modern life that a quarter of parents split up before their children are 16 years old. When parents divorce or separate, they often say, 'it's for the sake of the children,' but sometimes it is the children who suffer the most. They may feel guilty or worried that they will 'lose' the parent they no longer live with; and they may feel furious about events. They may also feel isolated and become withdrawn. Because this really is a situation they cannot control, self-harming may bring them a sense of control. The Trotman title *Real Life Issues: Family Break-ups* looks at the issue in detail (see the Resources section).

DRUG USE

We saw in the previous chapter that drug use can seriously affect your state of mind. It can lead to psychosis and other problems and make existing mental health problems worse. These can bring a sense of despair and worthlessness, effectively lowering a person's self-esteem (see below), which can in turn lead to other forms of self-harm. Having a parent who is a drug user can also lead to children self-harming as a result of feeling neglected, afraid, ashamed of their parent, angry and alone.

LOW SELF-ESTEEM

This is one of the main causes cited time and time again by self-harmers. They feel they are not 'good enough' – and never will be. They're not thin enough/tall enough/clever enough/attractive enough/popular enough to ever be successful. All these negative thoughts have a direct impact on their emotional state, making them sad, fearful, angry and lonely. They might feel like screaming, but believe no one will hear them even if they do – so self-harming becomes their scream. The Trotman title *Real Life Issues: Confidence and Self-Esteem* gives practical advice on how you can boost both (see the Resources section).

STRESS

The teenage years are an extremely stressful time, when childhood is left behind and the responsibilities of adulthood approach. Parents want their children to do well academically, there is pressure to pass exams, decisions must be made about future careers, and constant assessment can make individuals feel they must give 101% all the time. If young men and women do not have someone they can talk to about any stress they may feel, someone to whom they can 'let off steam,' stress can simply overwhelm them. The Trotman title *Real Life Issues: Stress* contains some self-help tips to keep stress at manageable levels (see the Resources section).

COPYCAT HARMING

Some of the people who were interviewed for the *Truth Hurts* report said they self-harmed because they had a close friend who also self-harmed, but as most self-harmers keep their behaviour secret their friends will not know about it. However, peer pressure may influence some young people to copycat self-harm in order to keep in with a friend or group of friends who also self-harm.

CHAPTER THREE:

HOW TO SPOT A SELF-HARMER
Clues to show if people around you are self-harming

Many self-harmers will go to great lengths to give the impression that nothing is wrong and nothing out of the ordinary is going on.

Because self-harmers are so secretive about what they do it can be very difficult to tell exactly who is self-harming, or has the potential to self-harm. The *Truth Hurts* report says: 'In the vast majority of cases self-harm remains a hidden and secretive behaviour that can go on for a long time without being discovered. [Young people] are extremely reluctant to talk about their self-harm or what may be troubling them. Most family and friends are likely to be unaware that someone close to them has self-harmed.'

This was made abundantly clear in the findings of the *National Survey of Mental Health of Children and Adolescents in the UK* (Meltzer). The research found that parents were often completely unaware of incidents of self-harm that their children reported to the same study. Of the 4249 young people interviewed, 248 said they had hurt themselves, whereas only 78 of the parents interviewed said that their child had attempted to hurt, harm or kill themselves. Parents were unlikely to be aware that self-harm was happening.

There is no such thing as a typical self-harmer: they can be female or male, of any race or creed, and from any section of society. Charlotte Church's mother Maria recently revealed she has been self-harming for 17 years by cutting her arms and stomach with kitchen knives and razors. She says the harm releases her unbearable tension. Olympic gold medal winner Dame Kelly Holmes went through two months of self-harming a year before her win in the 2004 Olympics. She cut herself after injuries threatened to ruin her career.

Many self-harmers will go to great lengths to give the impression that nothing is wrong and nothing out of the ordinary is going on. However, there are certain signs that may give you a clue that a person is self-harming and needs some help. It must be stressed that if a friend does exhibit any of the behaviours below it doesn't necessarily mean they are self-harming – they may just be going through a bad patch or a difficult time – but you may like to keep an eye on them.

STRESS

As we saw in the previous chapter, for many people self-harming is a way of dealing with unbearable levels of stress, and hurting themselves in secret may not be the only way the stress manifests itself. They may also:

- constantly scratch or pick at their skin, pull at their hair and bite their fingernails excessively
- start smoking heavily

- try to lose themselves by drinking alcohol, especially binge-drinking
- start misusing drugs such as cannabis.

You may find the Trotman title *Real Life Issues: Addictions* can help address drug and drink problems (see the Resources section at the end of this book).

APPEARANCE

Most self-harmers will go to great lengths to hide what they do. They may:

- become reluctant to take part in any activity that involves uncovering parts of their body: they may make excuses for missing PE, or find reasons not to go swimming or play sports
- start to change the way they dress, wearing long-sleeved tops and trousers even on sunny days: they may choose nondescript, many-layered or baggy clothes that make them feel they are 'invisible' and are not drawing attention to themselves
- appear subdued and withdrawn, and reluctant to make eye contact with you when you speak to them (staring at the floor or hiding their face with their hair), where once they were outgoing and lively
- become evasive, defensive and even aggressive if asked about any marks of injuries – unexplained bruises, cuts or burns – they may have.

MENTAL STATE

Self-harmers are in emotional pain, so their state of mind is often fragile. This may become apparent in a number of ways.

- Low self-esteem. Self-harmers believe they are worthless, that they don't count and that their opinions don't matter. Some come to believe their self-harming is all their own fault, that they have somehow brought it on themselves, because they are wicked or have done something wrong. Low self-esteem can lead to ...

- Poor functioning at school. Self-harmers may find it difficult to concentrate on their studies and their grades may dip significantly.
- Because they have so much else on their minds and they feel no one else can help them with this terrible secret they may become withdrawn or uninterested, lonely and isolated.
- Self-harmers exist in their own little world of pain and anger, which may make it difficult for them to handle feelings and emotions. They become so locked into the cycle of a build-up of pressure, its release through self-harm, then another build-up of pressure, that they seem to lose the ability to cope with other emotions.

OTHER FACTORS

Many of the factors listed above (low self-esteem, drug use in the past year, a high level of stress) were cited in the *Child and Adolescent Self-Harm in Europe* (CASE) study as significant causes of self-harm. The study also found two other significant factors associated with self-harm: if a family member or a close friend had attempted suicide or deliberately harmed themselves at some point in the young person's life; and if they had worries about their sexual orientation.

No one is really sure why exposure to suicide should influence vulnerable young people to harm themselves or attempt to take their own lives, but if you know someone who has recently been bereaved through suicide you should watch out for the signs listed above. You may find giving them a copy of the Trotman title *Real Life Issues: Bereavement* can help them come to terms with the grief (see the Resources section).

Young people are also very vulnerable when they are confused or worried about their sexuality. They often feel in need of support that is just not there. If you know someone who has recently come out, or is considering doing so, watch to see if they display any of the signs listed above.

Finally, look out for any major changes in behaviour, especially if a friend or schoolmate starts carrying around things like razors, cigarette lighters, or sharp objects they normally would not have on them.

WHAT YOU CAN DO IF YOU THINK SOMEONE YOU KNOW IS SELF-HARMING

If you do believe a friend or family member is self-harming, it is best not to confront them. Most self-harmers feel terrible shame at what they do, so they will deny it and continue to deny it, even if you ask them straight out. What most self-harmers really need is someone to talk to, someone who will really hear what they have to say, so the best way you can help is by **listening**. Ask them if they are OK or if they're feeling down and whether they'd like to talk about it. Then make sure you really concentrate on what they are saying. Even if they don't tell you everything that's worrying them, having a sympathetic ear can ease their pain and make them feel less isolated and alone.

If they do open up and confess to self-harming, try to be **non-judgemental**. Their behaviour may make you angry, and you may not understand why they are self-harming, but they feel bad enough about it already and if you start to criticise them it will only make them feel

'Having a friend who is there for me, who listens to me and supports me has made a huge difference to my self-harming. I don't know what I would have done without her.'

worse. Don't accuse them of being selfish, or even mad: they won't open up to you – or anyone else – if they think they'll be ridiculed.

There are also lots of practical things you can do to help them. First of all help them to **find information** – in books like this one, leaflets and websites. Trotman publishes a whole series of *Real Life Issues* books (you can find the relevant information on publications in the Resources section). You can encourage them to get **professional help**, and if they feel unable to do this themselves you could **offer to tell someone on their behalf**. If they do agree to go and see someone, offer to go with them as **moral support**.

Finally, **don't ask them to make promises they cannot keep**. Most self-harmers really, really want to stop what they are doing but have no alternative method of coping. As you will see in Chapter 6 it can take years for them to leave this behaviour behind them, so don't make them promise to stop – each time they break that promise it will make them feel wretched.

Being the friend of someone who self-harms can be difficult, so it will help you to have someone else to confide in. You don't have to give away your friend's secret if they don't want you to – you can just talk about them in the abstract: 'a person my sister knows;' or 'I know someone who knows someone who self-harms.'

If you feel it is more of a burden than you can bear, or if this is something you really don't want to face, be totally honest and tell your friend. Maybe you can suggest someone else they could tell. This doesn't mean you are no longer their ally and mate – on the contrary, it shows you care enough about them to want them to get the best possible help and advice from someone who knows how to deal with the situation.

CHAPTER FOUR:

STOPPING THE CYCLE OF SELF-HARM
Practical ways to help yourself or others stop self-harming

'*Stopping hurting myself was the hardest thing, but now I'm coping with the emotional pain in other ways I'm so much happier.*'

When the only way you can deal with emotional distress is to harm yourself, it can seem impossible to give up your coping method or release valve. This may be the one thing in your life you feel you have absolute control over, the one thing that stops you from exploding. But, as Max O'Neill says, self-harm can only ever offer a temporary release and it does not tackle the deep-seated problems that cause the motivation to self-harm. If these problems are not addressed the self-harm often escalates, so finding some other mechanism to help you cope is vital. In Chapter 5 you will find information about the many formal and informal bodies and associations you can turn to for help.

But as the young people who contributed to the *Truth Hurts* report emphasised, self-help is critical. This chapter describes the many different methods young self-harmers themselves have found useful in helping them to cope.

DISTRACTION TECHNIQUES

For many self-harmers the way to start coping with and managing their self-harm is to find something to distract them, even for a short time. Although distraction probably won't stop the self-harming completely it is a positive step towards recovery. Not all the methods listed below will work for everybody: the key is to find one (or a combination) you are comfortable with and that works for you. However, the first step to all of these techniques is to learn to recognise when the pressure inside you is becoming unbearable and act before the urge to self-harm can't be stopped.

Surf the urge

This is also known as the **five-minute rule**. If you start to feel that you want to self-harm, just wait for five minutes. If you manage the first five minutes successfully, see if you can go another five minutes. Eventually you will find you have 'surfed the urge' and the urge has gone.

Some people find counting down from ten to zero very slowly helps them to focus on something outside their pain. Alternatively, you could try slowing down your breathing: breathe in for a count of five; hold for one count; then breathe out for a count of five.

Waiting it out in this way can be very difficult for some people, but it can be done – especially if you combine it with one of the other self-help techniques below.

Talk is good

Waiting five minutes while your emotions are running riot can be agony. Filling the time with something else will help the time pass more quickly. Talking to someone is always a good thing – a problem shared is a problem halved – and you don't even have to talk about your self-harming: talk about anything you want to.

If you want to talk to someone in confidence you can ring helplines such as Childline or the Samaritans or one of the many self-help groups listed in the next chapter and in the Resources section at the end of this book. If you'd like a more informal chat, why not phone a friend and talk about school or music or films or anything else that will take your mind off self-harming? If you are in a situation where other people are around, see if you can talk to them face to face: a friend, your mum, dad or other family member, or even a teacher who you feel you can trust.

Write it out

Not everybody is good at talking: some people find it easier to express themselves by writing down what they feel. At the time, what you actually write is less important than the physical distraction of the writing itself: it is only later, when you reread what you have written, that you can use it to help manage your self-harming. Your writing can take many different forms.

KEEP A DIARY

'Very often young people do not have the words or emotional maturity to be able to deal with their issues through talking,' says Max O'Neill. 'If they don't, then keeping a Thought Diary can be really useful.' This is an exercise in which his patients write down a situation when they have self-harmed in the past. 'I ask them to write down what the situation was and what was it they thought,' he says. 'Then they write down what they subsequently did and how it felt. This way they can pinpoint what triggers them to self-harm. Over time they come to recognise when *this* happens then they think *this* and go on to self-harm.'

Some people keep a Mood Diary in which they chart the way their emotions rise and fall throughout the day. This can be especially helpful: a record of what your possible triggers are and how they affect you may help you to deal with them more positively in the future. One young girl discovered from her diary that her self-harming became worse at certain times during her menstrual cycle, so she was able to take measures to help relieve the symptoms of PMS (pre-menstrual syndrome) that were contributing to her self-harm. (See the section, 'Look after yourself', on page 34)

WRITE POETRY

Poetry is a distillation of feelings or thoughts – it can be raw, naked and bracingly honest. For many people who have no other ways of expressing their pain poetry can be a valuable release. One young man found writing song lyrics was his way of getting his hurt onto paper.

WRITE NOTES

When things are really bad and you are at a very low ebb, you may find the following technique brings some relief. If you're thinking 'I'm worthless' or 'I hate that bully at school' or 'I can't stand it any more,' write that thought down on a piece of paper. Now destroy the note by erasing or scribbling all over it, ripping it up into tiny pieces, putting it into a fire or setting light to it. Destroying the piece of paper helps you to destroy the negative thought.

Lose yourself in music

Music can be amazingly therapeutic. It often sums up our emotions perfectly, even when we can't put into words exactly what those feelings are. Some songs make us feel happy, some make us sad, others reflect our anger or pain. Often, when we feel most alone there is a piece of music, a band, one song or a whole CD that sums up what we feel and shows us other people feel the same way too. So make up a CD or download your favourite tracks onto your MP3 player, then sing along at the top of your voice. If you play a musical instrument, play that frustration and fury out. As one young self-harmer says, 'playing guitar makes me feel worthy.' If you're not particularly musical you may find making a loud noise by banging pots or pans, or screaming and shouting into a pillow helps relieve pent-up emotions.

Draw a picture

Art therapy is helpful for many people who have negative or even suicidal thoughts. Max O'Neill asks some of his patients to 'draw the feeling' with coloured pencils and pens. He says the results can be startling. 'Quite often by drawing what they are feeling they get a huge insight as to what is actually going on inside of them.'

Another thing many self-harmers find useful is to **draw on themselves** instead of physically damaging themselves. They take a red felt tip or marker pen and use it to draw on their body where they would otherwise cut or burn. The mark then becomes a symbolic scar that shows the pain they were feeling but doesn't leave a permanent mark. Others find putting a sticking plaster over the area of skin they intended to self-harm has the same symbolic effect.

Ice it

One way of mimicking the feeling cutting or burning can give you is by using an ice cube. Either hold the ice cube in your fist and slowly let it melt, giving a feeling of release as it does so, or rub it against the area of skin you would normally hurt. While melting ice produces a burning sensation, putting a rubber band around the wrist and repeatedly flicking it can produce a stinging sensation. Once again, these methods of distraction may help you to surf the urge.

Punch it out

Rather than taking your anger and frustration out on yourself, you could try turning it on an inanimate object such as a pillow or a punch bag. Try lining up a set of cushions, each representing a person who has caused or is causing you harm.

Now kick or punch the cushions in turn. As you do so, think about how each person has hurt you and how you do not deserve that hurt.

Act it out

Some therapists recommend drama therapy to their self-harming patients. If you like drama you may find it works on many levels. First, if you are improvising you can 'act out' your anger, your frustration and your pain. Second, if your role is a person who is very different from yourself, you can 'lose' yourself in that character, distracting yourself from your own problems for a while. Third, joining a drama group – either at school or in your home community – means you will be meeting and interacting with other people. This can help ease the terrible feeling of isolation and loneliness that many self-harmers feel.

Do some exercise

 You will also meet other people if you take up a team sport such as netball, football, hockey, rugby or basketball, or if you join a tennis or running club. You'll get out and about and socialise more – and exercise itself is good for you. Any form of exercise can help relieve the symptoms of depression. When you exercise your brain releases the hormone serotonin (the same hormone that is released when you self-harm), which regulates mood, appetite and sleep cycles. The more you exercise, the more serotonin is released and the better you feel. This can be taken too far: many young people who self-harm through eating disorders, such as bulimia and anorexia, over-exercise in order to control their weight and to get a 'high' from the serotonin that is produced. However, sensible exercise is beneficial, so go jogging, have a swim or do an aerobic exercise class – whatever feels good to you. If you are concerned skimpy shorts or bathing costumes will reveal self-harming scars, choose a form of exercise for which you don't have to strip off.

LOOK AFTER YOURSELF

Exercise is a very positive way of looking after yourself, but there are other things you can do that will boost your self-esteem and make you physically and emotionally stronger and therefore better able to cope with your self-harming. These include:

Eating well

Eating junk food will not give you the nutrients you need to keep healthy and strong. Try to eat plenty of fresh fruit and vegetables, eat regularly and don't skip meals, and if at all possible eat with other people so you can sit and talk rather than eating alone.

Getting enough sleep

Lack of sleep can make you moody, short-tempered and less able to cope with everyday situations. If you are suffering from insomnia or disturbed sleep your doctor can prescribe medication that can help (but this should only be used as a short-term measure). Alternatively, you could try one of the herbal remedies that are available over the counter; or have a warm, relaxing bath or shower and/or a hot milky drink before you go to bed.

Boosting your immune system

Keep your immune system in tiptop shape by making sure you get enough vitamins and minerals. Zinc, in particular, is very good for both the immune system and for healthy skin. A vitamin or mineral supplement is easy to take in either pill or capsule form and if your self-harming takes the form of cutting or burning your skin it is really important as it will help your body's healing processes. If you are a girl who suffers badly from PMS that is causing violent mood swings, irrational behaviour and an increase in self-harming, natural remedies such as increasing your intake of the vitamin B6 (important for mood regulation) or taking a course of evening primrose oil may prove beneficial. According to a 2001 report the herb St John's wort has also proved helpful and has no side effects.

Building up your self-esteem

Most self-harmers have very low self-esteem: they think they are useless, worthless individuals. Over time these negative feelings begin to reinforce themselves until they become so ingrained that people feel they can never escape them. But you can escape them: the trick is to replace the negative with the positive. Whenever you find yourself thinking 'I hate myself, no one could ever love me,' replace it with a positive affirmation such as 'every day, in every way, I am getting better and better' or 'I am a worthwhile person who deserves to be happy and healthy.' Affirmations work best when they are repeated regularly, so in order to reinforce your own affirmations make a tape of your voice saying them and play it back to yourself every day or whenever you feel you need a boost.

> *'I had a relapse last week, but one setback doesn't mean I can't do this. I'm on the mend and things can only get better.'*

Being gentle with yourself

Remember, you self-harm for a reason; you do it in order to cope with the terrible pain and pressure you feel inside. It is your survival mechanism, so don't be hard on yourself. Give yourself occasional treats, be gentle with yourself and if you only manage to distract yourself for five minutes for one day then give yourself a pat on the back – you have taken the first step to tackling your self-harming.

WHO CAN I TURN TO?
Where to get information and advice

'Getting help was the best thing I ever did and my advice to anyone else who self-harms is go and find someone who you can talk to, who can help you, you'll feel so much better.'

People who do not self-harm sometimes find it difficult to understand why those who do don't immediately seek help to overcome it. Unfortunately, because self-harm is still something of a taboo subject it isn't often talked about openly – and this means there is still a lot of ignorance surrounding the subject.

But ignorance is only one reason self-harmers don't seek the help they so desperately crave. Some don't come forward because they are ashamed of what they do. It makes them feel guilty and even the thought of talking to someone else about it fills them with dread. Others are afraid that if they admit to their self-harm they will lose control of it, that the people they tell will 'take over' and this will further erode what little control they feel they have over their lives. There may also be an element of mistrust: self-harmers worry that their 'secret' will not be kept confidential and people they don't want to know will find out about it. Some are afraid that they will be labelled 'mad' and be forced into a psychiatric ward or hospital for treatment they do not want. Others are worried people in authority will dismiss them as time-wasters who don't really have a problem at all but are just seeking attention.

But probably the major reason for young people not seeking help for self-harming is that they simply don't know who to talk to, where to go, or what options are available to them.

WHO, WHAT, WHERE

There are plenty of people out there who do want to help and who are specifically trained to help. They will respect your right to privacy and treat you with sensitivity. There are also many former self-harmers, along with others who still self-harm, who have come together in informal groups offering mutual support. What type of help you decide to get will very much depend on what your personal circumstances are and what you feel comfortable with.

FIRST STEPS

During the research stage of the *Truth Hurts* report young people were asked: 'What do you think could be done to help prevent young people from feeling that they want to hurt themselves?' Most of the respondents (over 25%) said someone who would listen to them, and give advice and support. Interestingly, the respondents were three times more likely to suggest talking to friends or family members than approaching formal bodies, so it would seem that for most young people at risk from self-harm, talking to family or other people they already know would be the first step to getting help.

However, 7% (mainly girls) suggested that it would be useful to have someone in school to give advice and support and that approaching a teacher, school counsellor, school peer group or school nurse could also be an option.

People who self-harm were asked what sort of help they would want to be available. The most popular responses were face-to-face/one-to-one support (such as counselling) and group support (such as drop ins and self-help groups) However, new technologies such as multimedia/internet access are increasingly being used, especially by boys who traditionally tend to shy away from face-to-face interaction and feel more comfortable accessing information via websites.

If you are not close to your family, or there has been family breakdown, abuse or trauma, or if you have no one close to talk to, the school peer group, professional counselling or a self-help group may suit your needs better. Take a look at the diagram on the next page to see just what variety of support and advice is on offer.

FAMILY MEMBERS/ FRIENDS

As we saw in the previous chapter, talking can be the first step on the path to recovery. If you feel you can't talk to your mum or dad, or if they are not there for you, then you may want to talk to a friend you feel you can confide in. However, you don't necessarily need to actually admit to your self-harming or talk about it specifically – just discussing your day or what has happened at school, or saying that

Who can I turn to?

Close family members: mother/father/ brother/sister

Other family members: grandparent aunt/uncle/ cousin

Websites/ internet forums

Friends/ acquaintances

Counselling: one-to-one/ group

School teacher/ school nurse/ school peer group

Self-help groups/support groups

GP/CAMHS (Child and Adolescent Mental Health Services)

Telephone helplines: Childline/ Samaritans/ Saneline

you're feeling under pressure, can give an enormous sense of relief and release.

SCHOOL

If the pressure of schoolwork or exams is one of the reasons you are finding it difficult to cope, do talk to your teacher or school counsellor about it. Once again, you don't necessarily need to talk about your self-harming specifically, just say that you're having problems. However, if

'Talking to people about the way I feel, or about what I've seen on TV, makes me feel calmer and helps the urge to hurt myself go away.'

you do mention self-harming your teacher or counsellor should be able to offer support and put you in contact with a person who is qualified to help.

Peer support groups

Many young people find talking to an adult about such personal things a little bit intimidating and they prefer to talk to people their own age. This is why peer support groups are so popular and why many schools now have them in place. Discovering that others are facing the same stresses and pressures can be very comforting, and listening to how they have successfully dealt with them may give you an insight into how you can learn to cope without the need to self-harm.

During Anti-Bullying Week last year, the government announced plans to expand its 'peer mentoring' scheme for schoolchildren. It was announced a further £480,000 will be spent on the scheme, which encourages schools to elect pupil representatives to help crack down on bullying.

The elected representatives take on the responsibility of helping teachers maintain good behaviour, prevent bullying and monitor pupil safety. Two very successful peer support schemes – Place2Be and Chips – are helping young people to help themselves.

The Place2Be

The Place2Be is committed to providing support to troubled, unhappy children in schools. The charity was founded in 1994 in response to increasing concern about the extent and depth of emotional and behavioural difficulties displayed in classrooms and playgrounds.

Some of the most common worries include parental divorce and separation, drug/alcohol-related problems, family illness, bereavement/loss, bullying, transfer to a new school, domestic violence, neglect, self-harm and physical or sexual abuse.

The Place2Be is currently available to 37,000 children in 112 schools across the UK. The charity's 100 qualified professional staff and 350 trained volunteer counsellors provide counselling in the dedicated Place2Be room (a 'safe space') in each school. Children can access one-to-one support or group work, or visit the lunchtime drop-in service, and take part in class and assembly sessions. Support for school staff and parents is also available and a range of accredited training programmes for the wider childcare workforce has been developed, based on the organisation's practical experience of enabling therapeutic and emotional support in schools.

The Place2Be has been notably successful in working with young males, who are usually unwilling to engage in support services, particularly those concerned with emotional health and well being. Boys like 7-year-old Alfie, who had endured three years of abuse by a 'family friend.' It was only when Alfie's mum found him in his bedroom stabbing his head with a fork that she uncovered the truth about the abuse. Soon after, Alfie began working with his Place2Be counsellor. At first he remained withdrawn and was very wary. Gradually as the weeks progressed he became more confident in his play, using toy farm animals to explore feelings of hurt and fear. By the end of the year Alfie was far more outgoing and able to cope with school life. Mum said 'Alfie is like a different boy. He's happier, chattier, has friends and plays out like a normal boy.'

The Place2Be, Wapping Telephone Exchange,
Royal Mint Street, London E1 8LQ
Tel: 020 7780 6189   Email: enquiries@theplace2be.org.uk

CHIPS

Since 1998 Childline in Partnerships (CHIPS) has brought Childline – the UK's free, 24-hour, confidential helpline for children – into direct contact with thousands of UK schools, youth clubs and other youth organisations. CHIPS helps schools and youth groups set up peer support schemes that give young people the opportunity to help one another and develop practical communication skills.

In 2005/2006 CHIPS worked with over 75,000 children and young people across 998 schools, youth clubs and other organisations in the UK. CHIPS is also beginning to develop services and resources to help specialist and hard-to-reach groups of young people, such as deaf children and those with learning difficulties.

The CHIPS programme raises awareness about Childline's work and the issues young people face. It does this through organising presentations, workshops and conferences for education professionals. CHIPS also provides an opportunity for a network of schools to share ideas and good practice, through regular mailings, and the newsletter *CHIPS Chat*.

Most of the CHIPS training covers generic counselling skills such as empathetic listening as well as principles like confidentiality. Self-harm is only one aspect of any training provided, although Head of CHIPS Lindsay Gilbert reports that it is something many peer supporters often specifically ask about. One case study in their six hour training programme tackles the issue – which is still a difficult one for many schools. Participants are asked what the concept means to them, and trainers emphasise that it is not a failed suicide bid but often a way of relieving pressure. A group of young people who self-harm have also planned and provided an advanced training day on the topic for the use of peer supporters.

Source: CHIPS/NSPCC (with permission)

GP/CAMHS (CHILD AND ADOLESCENT MENTAL HEALTH SERVICES)

If you decide to go to your GP, or if you self-harm so badly that you need to go to hospital, the National Institute for Clinical Excellence (NICE) has guidelines on self-harm that specifically address the needs of young people (see the box opposite). If you go to see your GP for treatment for a self-inflicted injury NICE recommends she/he should talk to you in confidence in an atmosphere of respect and understanding and should also offer you a full assessment of your physical, psychological and social needs. This is also the case if you have to go to hospital for a more serious injury.

CAMHS

If you are under 18 years old you can get support and treatment through the Child and Adolescent Mental Health Services. Your GP or school nurse can refer you to CAMHS or you can contact them via GP surgeries, at health centres and hospitals and at some schools, colleges, universities and youth centres. What treatment and help they offer will depend on which local health service they're in, but they all have specialist staff (some have specially trained nurses) who can offer assessment and then treatment geared to your needs. For more information on CAMHS see the Resources section at the end of this book.

HELPLINES

Because they are so easily accessible and widely known, telephone helplines are a popular source of confidential support. Services such as Childline and the Samaritans allow you to talk to somebody anonymously and in private.

The number of children talking to Childline's counsellors about self-harm has grown steadily over the last ten years. Between 2002 and

NICE Guidelines on Self-Harm 2004

Professionals treating you for self-injury or self-poisoning should be sensitive about your ability to communicate. Staff should give you the opportunity to explain your feelings and understanding about your self-harm in your own words. If you go to an emergency department, the healthcare professional you see should discuss with you where you would like to wait and whether you would like a member of staff to sit with you. The environment should feel safe and supportive, and you should be told the name of the member of staff looking after you while you wait. Wherever possible, you should be offered the choice of male or female staff for both treatment and assessment. When this is not possible, the reasons should be explained to you and written in your notes.

Sometimes people who injure themselves will be offered treatment by their GP without referral for further physical treatment. If you do go to see someone in your general practice, you should be offered a full assessment that includes your physical, psychological and social needs. This should be done by a trained professional at the earliest opportunity and in an atmosphere of respect and understanding. If you do see someone, your doctor should respect your right to privacy, but this does depend on your age and how unwell you are. Your parents or your guardian should ideally be told about the assessment.

To view the complete NICE guidelines, visit www.nice.org.uk

2003 Childline heard from over 3000 children and young people who said they were self-harming or had self-harmed. If you're feeling that no one will listen sympathetically to what you have to say or take it seriously, these helplines can act (as the *Truth Hurts* report said) as a 'friendly listening ear.' They can also direct you to other organisations that work with young people who self-harm. See the Resources section for a list of telephone helplines.

SELF-HELP SUPPORT GROUPS

Self-help groups offer mutual support to both former self-harmers and those who are still self-harming. Regularly talking to people who have experienced what you are going through allows you to explore your feelings about self-harm, the reasons behind it, and the mechanisms you can put in place in order to cope with it. If you are feeling isolated these groups give you the opportunity to form friendships, learn to trust other people and begin to share and explore common experiences and knowledge.

In 2003, the Mental Health Foundation commissioned research into the positive and negative effects of attending a self-harm self-help group. The findings showed self-help groups offer a safe place to talk openly and honestly without fearing the response from professionals. Although some professionals themselves are rather cautious about these groups – they worry that talking about self-harm to other people who self-harm may encourage people to continue – many of the people who took part in the research stressed the helpfulness of contact with others who self-harmed and how this had been the turning point in their own recovery.

Your local Mind association or MindInfoLine (0845 766 0163) will have information on local self-help groups. If there is no group in your area Mind may be able to help you start one. For more contacts see the Resources section.

COUNSELLING

For many young people who self-harm, counselling (or therapy) – either in a group or singly – can be a godsend. As Max O'Neill points out: 'Very often, being in therapy is the only time young people get to talk about themselves in a way where they are not judged.' In recent years there has been an increase in the availability of counselling services across the NHS and the voluntary sector, and if you would rather talk to someone who is not connected to you or your family this may be the type of help you would prefer.

Counselling comes in many forms, including cognitive behaviour therapy (CBT) and hypnotherapy, and the reason it is effective is because it strives to get to the root causes of why you harm yourself and deal with those issues rather than just treat the symptoms. 'Unless you actually deal with what is causing the emotional distress you are never going to break the cycle,' says Max O'Neill. A trained counsellor will help you access your true feelings and work on giving you new methods for dealing with them.

The NICE guidelines recommend that 'such treatment (therapy) should last for at least three months. Psychological therapies will aim to address the underlying reasons why you harm yourself, and how you feel when you hurt yourself.'

Your GP can give you details of counselling services in your area, as can the British Association of Counselling and Psychotherapy (BACP) listed in the Resources section.

'I've found a counsellor I like, and he has made me realise my self-harming is a way of expressing my inner frustration and anger. Talking to him calms me and although I still want to cut, I no longer actually need to.'

WEBSITES/INTERNET FORUMS

Although there are many incredibly helpful and informative websites and internet forums about self-harm, others are less so. Once again, some professionals worry they may actually encourage people to continue to self-harm. However, the fact that they can be accessed easily and anonymously makes them an attractive option. Young men, who traditionally don't like to ask for help because it is thought 'unmanly,' find websites especially helpful. There is a list of websites in the Resources section.

CHAPTER SIX:

THE ROAD TO RECOVERY
Breaking the cycle and moving on

'With the help of a support group I'm learning new ways of dealing with my pain. I still self-harm, but less and less frequently and now I actually feel hope for the future.'

For the majority of young people who self-harm as a result of a specific problem or pressure, the urge to hurt themselves recedes as the problem or pressure recedes. When their 'trigger' is removed, the pressure no longer builds up, so they no longer feel the need to self-harm.

Other young people reduce and stop their self-harm more gradually over time. This may happen because they escape from bullying situations after moving home or changing schools, or finish their exams, or go to university. A gradual reduction of self-harm is particularly common in young people whose self-harm stems from multiple and connected causes, such as being picked on at school and having low self-esteem, or having a difficult home life and no one to talk to. Once one or more of these factors are removed, they may no longer feel they have to use self-harm as a coping strategy.

Some self-harmers manage to break the cycle without any help from professionals or self-help organisations. But those who self-harm more habitually can find the road to recovery much longer and more difficult. They may need to seek counselling or join self-help groups to learn new strategies for coping before they can give up the only method of coping they know – self-harm. Part of this process will involve looking deep within themselves to discover the root causes of their behaviour, and this can be very distressing, especially if they have been victims of abuse. It can take weeks or months (the NICE guidelines say counselling should last at least three months), during which they reduce the instances of self-harm; but some find it impossible to stop entirely until they are healed emotionally. However, to someone who previously could only find relief by hurting their own body, even a reduction in episodes can seem like a huge victory.

This is where health professionals and self-harmers seem to differ in their interpretation of what is meant by 'recovery.' The *Truth Hurts* report states: 'The Inquiry recognised the need to clarify what is meant by recovery in terms of self-harm. Some young people interpret it as reducing their self-harm as they tackle the underlying issues, using distraction techniques and minimising the damage that self-harm inflicts; others interpret it as completely stopping self-harm. Professionals in particular need to be clear that many young people use the first interpretation.'

This difference in interpretation can cause difficulties, especially for front-line health professionals trying to do the best they can for their patients. At the Royal College of Nursing's (RCN) Congress in April 2006 nurses debated whether they should allow patients to practise 'safe' self-harm (see the box below). This could involve giving self-harm patients sterile blades and clean packets of bandages or ensuring that they keep their own blades clean and giving patients advice about which parts of the body it is least dangerous to cut. At present nurses are expected to stop anyone doing physical harm to themselves and to confiscate any sharp objects (e.g. razor blades, broken glass or tin cans).

Ian Hulatt, Mental Health Adviser for the RCN, said: 'Nurses who encounter individuals who self-harm on a regular basis face a dilemma. Do they go for prohibition? Or do we allow this to occur in a way that minimises harm? Some nurses will not support this because our code of practice says we should not do patients any harm. But this may be less harmful than patients using dirty implements. There are mental health units that already allow the use of sterile implements.'

Safe Self-Harm Debate: RCN Congress 2006

Deliberate self-harm is a common phenomenon that challenges healthcare service providers. For some individuals this behaviour is impulsive and limited, for some it's life threatening, and for others it is a means of managing distress. Nurses face a particular challenge from the latter group, often being in the position of advising how to self-harm safely.

Recent NICE guidance (National Institute for Clinical Excellence, 2004) emphasises that staff who encounter people who self-harm should do so in a manner that is not perceived as punitive. Whilst these guidelines are clearly restricted to the care and treatment of individuals in the first 48 hours following an episode of self-harm, it is in other environments that the challenges occur. These guidelines build upon national strategies on suicide and self-harm in both England and Scotland.

Nurses who promote safety to self-harmers may fear they are in contravention of their Code of Conduct, which requires that 'As a registered nurse, midwife or specialist community public health nurse, you must act to identify and minimise the risk to patients and clients' (Nursing and Midwifery Council, 2004). While individual nurses may feel constrained by their Code of Conduct, trusts seem anxious about the possibility of litigation and may determine that under no circumstances should promotion of safety to self-harmers be permitted. This leaves the nurse in a difficult position. Encouraging complete abstention from self-harm and not promoting safety may precipitate a worsening of the client's condition or at least deterioration in their relationship with the client. Parallels could be drawn with those individuals who self-harm via drug use. It is established practice to encourage an ethos of harm reduction and providing sterile syringes and needles is considered safe and appropriate practice. This was a development that was similarly controversial when initiated.

The RCN has been meeting with the NMC to discuss safe self-harm and the impact the Code of Conduct has upon this issue of practice. Discussions have focused on ways of working with self-harm and service user views. This work remains ongoing.

Nurses engage with thousands of individuals every year who engage in episodes of self-harm. Many are single events that may not be repeated, while some service users utilise deliberate self-harm strategies such as cutting as a means of managing their mental distress. This may be a long and well-established pattern of self-management and any insistence on total abstention may cause the individual further distress.

Source: Royal College of Nursing (RCN) (with permission)

MANAGED SELF-HARM/ HARM MINIMISATION

Many young people believe they are on the road to recovery from the point when they get help for their problem – even if, at that point, they are still self-harming. The way they see it is that they are no longer in denial, they have acknowledged their problem, and this is the first step towards addressing that problem. Max O'Neill agrees: 'The very fact a patient keeps coming back to (counselling) sessions is a victory of sorts in itself, because although they may still self-harm in their everyday lives, while they are talking about their behaviour with me they are not self-harming. I think quite often managing self-harm is about damage limitation.'

As the self-harmer learns new, healthier coping strategies, self-harming episodes occur less often and are less severe (the cuts become more superficial, individuals may still fuss with their hair but no longer pull it out). 'Part of the work we do with them is reframing their negative belief system ("I'll never be good enough, I feel no hope for the future") with a more positive one so from a place where they feel powerless they realise they can take back the control and power in their lives and they can take responsibility for what happens to them.'

'It's funny but before, when I was self-harming, I didn't care about the future because I was in such despair. But now I do care, I care enough to want to get well and stay well. I never want to go back to that black place again.'

DEALING WITH SCARS (EMOTIONAL AND PHYSICAL)

When self-harmers start out on the road to recovery they feel like anyone who is recovering from an illness: they start to feel better in themselves and they become more energetic. Where once they may have wanted to be self-contained, now they want to engage with the world more and they become interested in life again. One element of this recovery may well be a renewed attention to their appearance. As the need to remain anonymous or 'hidden' disappears they may feel like wearing more revealing clothes.

However, one of the lasting legacies of self-harming is scars, and physical scars are immediately visible. Some people may see their scars as a badge of honour (one of Max O'Neill's patients told him: 'my scars are a visible reminder for me that I'm coping. Each scar tells a story – when it got this bad I was able to relieve the pressure by making this scar'), but others are deeply distressed and ashamed by them. Part of their process of recovery is learning how to deal with existing scars by accepting them as part of who they are – and by realising these are scars they no longer need to reopen in order to get on with their lives.

It's also possible to get help to camouflage the scars with make-up. Some people find this very reassuring because it makes them feel more 'normal' and therefore more comfortable in social situations like going to school, to the shops or the cinema. Both the British Red Cross and the Skin Camouflage Network can offer help and advice on physical scarring. (For more information see the Resources section.)

Feeling comfortable with the way you look can make you feel generally better in yourself because it boosts your confidence, but there are other positive things you can do for yourself on the road to recovery to make you feel stronger and more hopeful.

Give it time

Don't expect the urge to self-harm to disappear overnight; and do expect there to be setbacks when you are feeling very stressed. When this happens, don't despair. Look at each day as another step along the road to recovery – you may only be taking small steps, but you are heading in the right direction.

Be good to yourself

Give yourself a pat on the back. You've been through a lot of pain and you've survived. As you start to feel better give yourself little treats – try listening to music, going to the cinema, enjoying time with people who appreciate you, people you don't have to compete with, people whose company you feel comfortable in.

Get involved

One of the best things you can do as your confidence increases is to get involved with other people in some way. This will take your mind off your own problems, get you out of the house (probably the place where self-harm usually occurs) and give you a focus. What about joining a sports club? Do you feel strong enough to join a self-help group? Does your school have a peer group where – if you feel up to it – you could use your own experiences to help others?

'While I was self-harming I thought it would be easy to stop, but it hasn't been. But I try to stay active and I'm still talking to someone about my behaviour because now I know there is another way. I am getting through it and that makes me feel so much happier.'

Keep talking!

Remember, at any one time two children in every secondary school classroom in the UK will be self-harming, so if you are a self-harmer YOU ARE NOT ALONE. There are many people out there going through what you are going through, so don't feel you have to suffer in silence. Do talk to someone, even if it is just about how your day has been rather than specifically about your self-harming. The more you talk the more you will be distracted from the urge to self-harm and the more you will be able to put your problems into perspective.

CONCLUSION

At the beginning of this book we quoted some worrying statistics about the number of young people in Britain who self-harm. It seems our modern world has become so stressful many individuals cannot function normally day to day. 'Just negotiating life in general is difficult for young people and it is getting harder,' says Max O'Neill. 'We only have to look at what is going on in society as a whole to see where the problems lie. If we look at the divorce rates and the number of relationships that irrevocably break down; the fact adolescents are disengaging from society spending hours watching TV or on the internet so they don't have the interaction skills of previous generations; the fact they often don't have a positive role model and the media doesn't tend to portray young people in a positive light; and finally, the unbearable pressure to succeed at school; these all contribute to the fact young people are not coping, so they develop alternative coping strategies such as becoming part of a gang, experimenting with drugs, binge-drinking or self-harming.'

Although self-harm is not the healthiest or most effective way of coping, some young people find themselves in a place where it seems to be the *only* way: it is their method of surviving the great pain they feel. But there are other ways – and there are people who can help.

If you are a self-harmer the most important thing to remember is that you really do have choices, even if you think you don't. You can choose to continue to self-harm, or you can choose to stop self-injuring today. The very fact you've picked up this book in the first place could be your first step to a harm-free future. No one says stopping self-harming is easy, but it can be done.

Below are the words of some self-harmers who have chosen to be harm-free. Reading them may give you the courage to start believing in a future that is bright and full of hope.

'I want to tell people who may be going through what I've been through – please get help, there are people out there who will listen.'

'You'll be surprised at how good it feels to get it all out in the open.'

'Going through counselling was the best thing I ever did.'

'Talking to the Samaritans was the sounding board I needed to help me to stop self-harming. Now I'm on the up and I truly believe things will continue to get better.'

'I thought I was in control of my self-harming, now I realise it was controlling me and I'm not going to let it do that anymore.'

'Self-harming was making me live in the past but now I want to move forward, I want a better life for myself.'

RESOURCES

Basement Project
PO Box 5
Abergavenny NP7 5XW
Tel: 01873 856524
www.basementproject.co.uk
*Provides support groups for people who have been abused as children
and for people who self-harm.*

BBC Mental Health
www.bbc.co.uk.health/mental/
*This section of the BBC website provides a clearly written overview of
self-harm. Go to the homepage, look under Emotional Health and
click on Self-Harm. It also has sections on stress and eating disorders.*

British Association for Counselling and Psychotherapy (BACP)
BACP House
35–37 Albert Street
Rugby CV21 2SG
Tel: 0870 443 5252
www.bacp.co.uk

*If you believe you could be helped by visiting a counsellor or a
therapist, BACP can offer details of those practitioners working in the
area where you live. BACP is a professional body and will only put you
in contact with qualified practitioners.*

Campaign Against Living Miserably (CALM)

Tel (freephone): 0800 585858 (daily, 5pm to 3am)
www.thecalmzone.net

*CALM is specifically targeted at young men aged between 15 and 35,
but anyone can call their helpline. There are currently three
'CALMzones' around the country (in Manchester, Merseyside and
Bedfordshire), but you can call them wherever you live and they will
put you in touch with nationally available services. CALM's advisors
are all trained in counselling and the service is confidential.*

Child and Adolescent Mental Health Services (CAMHS)

www.camhs.org.uk

*This website provides links to professionals from health, local authority
and voluntary organisations.*

Childline

Freepost 1111
London N1 0BR
Tel (freephone): 0800 1111
Textphone: 0800 400222
www.childline.org.uk

*If you can't talk to anyone you know about what you are feeling but
need to discuss things with someone, contact Childline. Childline takes
young people's problems seriously, calls are confidential, and its
counsellors can offer advice about your local sources of help. The
telephone service is free and available 24/7. The website contains
information and advice on a range of problems experienced by young*

people, and it publishes an online booklet, Saving Young Lives: Calls to Childline About Suicide, *which includes information on self-harm problems at school; relationships; bullying; and eating problems.*

Connexions
Tel: 0808 001 3219
Text: 07766 413219
Textphone: 0800 096 8336
www.connexions-direct.com
Connexions Personal Advisers and Connexions Direct National Advisers are not trained counsellors, but they can talk you through what counselling is available. You can speak to a Personal Adviser at your local Connexions Centre. To find your local centre click on the Local Services icon at the bottom of the homepage or look in your local phone book.

Mental Health Foundation
Tel: 020 7803 1100
Email: mhf@mhf.org.uk
www.mentalhealth.org.uk
Published Truth Hurts: Report of the National Enquiry into Self-Harm Among Young People *(2006), a copy of which can be downloaded as a pdf file from the website. The Mental Health Foundation also publishes an information booklet entitled* The Truth About Self-Harm for Young People and Their Friends and Families *for those who want to know more about self-harm; what it is, why people do it, and where to go for help. The booklet is based on the experiences of young people who have self-harmed. For a copy of the free information booklet visit www.selfharmUK.org.*

Mind

Tel: 0845 766 0163

www.mind.org.uk

Mind is the leading mental charity in England and Wales. Its website contains links to many articles on various aspects of mental health. If you are worried that a friend might have suicidal tendencies its free booklet How to Help Someone Who is Feeling Suicidal *will prove useful. It also publishes* The Mind Guide To Managing Stress.

National Children's Bureau

www.selfharm.org.uk

This is a detailed website containing everything you need to know about self-harming written in a no-nonsense style, complete with links to organisations and other websites.

National Institute for Clinical Excellence (NICE)

Email: selfharm@nice.nhs.uk

www.nice.org.uk

NICE issues clinical guidelines for practitioners, including doctors and nurses, on how they should treat patients who self-harm. You can view these on NICE's website.

National Self-Harm Network

PO Box 7246

Nottingham NG1 6WJ

Email: info@nshn.co.uk

www.nshn.co.uk

This organisation offers information and support to people who self-harm and their friends, families and carers. It is run by people who have themselves survived self-harm.

Place2Be

Tel: 020 7780 6189

Email: enquiries@theplace2be.org.uk

The Place2Be currently works with 37,000 children over 112 schools in England and Scotland. It aims to provide early intervention service to children who have been abused, bullied, bereaved or who suffer from low self-esteem.

Recover Your Life

www.recoveryourlife.com

One of the largest of the online self-harm communities, Recover Your Life has forums, a live chat line and a community area. There are also sections on eating disorders and depression.

Samaritans

Tel: 0845 790 9090

Textphone: 0845 790 9192

www.samaritans.org

The Samaritans offer a confidential 24-hour service for anyone who wants to talk to one of their trained operators.

Saneline

Tel: 0845 767 8000

Saneline can direct you to sources of advice and help in your area or can just be a listening ear. It gets over 2500 calls every month and is open from 1pm to 11pm daily.

Self Harm Alliance (SHA)

PO Box 61

Cheltenham

Gloucestershire GL51 8YB

Email: selfharmalliance@aol.com

www.selfharmalliance.org
This is a survivor-led self-help resource.

siHelp

www.sihelp.co.uk
siHelp supports the friends and families of people who self-harm, and the website is packed with information.

YoungMinds

Tel: 020 7336 8445
Email: enquiries@youngminds.org.uk
www.youngminds.org.uk
This national charity is committed to improving the mental health of all young people. It issues a YoungMinds magazine and leaflets and booklets to help young people, including one on general depression. It has published a series of articles concerning self-harm. If you click on the Info section you will find links to other organisations that can help in the case of young people and self-harm.

FOR HELP WITH SCARRING

British Red Cross UK Office

44 Moorfields
London EC2Y 9Al
Tel: 020 7877 7000
The British Red Cross runs a scar camouflaging service and gives information on how you can diminish the look of scars.

Skin Camouflage Network

www.skincamouflagenetwork.org.uk
This is the site for the National Association of Practitioners of Skin Camouflage and can help in finding a skin camouflage clinic, either NHS or private, in your area.

SUPPORT FOR PEOPLE BEING BULLIED

Bullying Online

www.bullying.co.uk

Provides practical advice if you or someone you know is being bullied. This charity has 30 sections of practical advice that may help and is the UK's biggest bullying resource. It produced last year's Bullying Online survey.

SUPPORT FOR PEOPLE WITH EATING DISORDERS

Eating Disorders Association (EDA)

Tel (youth helpline): 0845 634 7650 (Monday–Friday, 4.30pm to 8.30pm; Saturday, 1pm to 4.30pm)

Email: talkback@edauk.com

www.edauk.com

The association provides information, help and support for people affected by eating disorders and, in particular, anorexia and bulimia nervosa. EDA offers a range of services, including national telephone helplines. Its Youth Helpline is for anyone under 18 years of age.

BOOKS

Trotman's *Real Life Issues* series

Self-help books offering information and advice on a range of key issues. Each book defines the issue and offers ways of understanding and coping with it. The following titles may be relevant and useful and are available from Trotman:

Bereavement, Dee Pilgrim (2006)

Confidence and Self-Esteem, Nicki Household (2004)

Coping with Life, Jonathan Bradley (2005)

Eating Disorders, Heather Warner (2004)
Family Break-ups, Adele Cherreson Cole (2006)
Stress, Rozina Breen (2004)